FLEET SALVAGE

I0107927

Natalie Sorrell Charlesworth is a Preston native. She won the *Poetic Republic Portfolio Prize* 2014, was specially commended in *Elbow Room* 2016, commended in *Hive* 2022, shortlisted for the *Bridport Poetry Prize* 2020 and longlisted for *Mslexia* 2021. Her work appears in *Poetic Republic, Elbow Room, Beautiful Dragons* and *Hidden Disabilities*. She is Digital Marketing and Social Media Executive for Solaris Books, an active board member for Lancaster Litfest, an artist and genealogist. *Fleet Salvage* is her debut pamphlet.

ISBN: 978-1-915760-25-8

The author has asserted their right to be identified as the author of this Work in accordance with the Copyright, Designs and Patents Act 1988

Cover designed by Aaron Kent

Edited and typeset by Aaron Kent

Broken Sleep Books Ltd
Rhydwen
Talgarreg
Ceredigion
SA44 4HB

Broken Sleep Books Ltd
Fair View
St Georges Road
Cornwall
PL26 7YH

Fleet Salvage

Natalie Sorrell Charlesworth

Broken Sleep Books

Contents

CENSUS-TAKING

Ghost-Walking

Dunoon Pier 26th June 1957

Ten years since last sight of you   you reappear
four feet in front of me   dawdling down the pier
        with an aspiring Hepburn and Loren
slingbacks snagging on the slats   wide polka dot skirts
sunglasses slipping   down your upturned noses
            three feet   past an anoraked grandfather
pipe trailing smoke like a steam train's chimney
    stroll a pair of celluloid starlets   and you
Dunoon's Glasgow-accented answer to Dorothy Dandridge
        cradling newsprint chips in the crook of your arm
licking your fingers after each bite   salt speckling
        the scarlet-slicked sheen of your lips
                        two feet   your laugh carries
there's a canted tilt to your chin   I never could fit
        to any family member living   one

   you've chemically straightened and set your hair
I miss the natural curve   the strength I had to learn
    to twist and tame it   into cornrows   or bantu knots
But your skin is the same   still two shades darker
        than milk splashed tea   you brush past
            apologise   glance back
    over your shoulder as you recede out of shot
your father's eyes appear darker   set in my face
        they remain blank   unknowing   I hang back
scuttle forward   dodging contortionists   unicyclists
    toffee apple hawkers   watch you weaving away
through the crowd   laughing   the turbulent wake
of other holidaymakers   conceals a tiny   headscarfed
woman with ease you leave the crowd   but
                I am bound to the boards

training the pier's telescope   on your silhouettes
       a string of paper dolls linked at the arms
I lose my shillings   willingly   one by one
as I chase your matchstick figure's stretching shadow
      juddering along the strandline
as if from   cell to cell   of unspooling film
      until the coins run out   you disappear
with the clacking wind-down of celluloid on capstan
I descend to the sand   linger in the lee of the pier's posts
neck craning for a better view   digging my fingers
into my bag's handle to quell the stretching itch in my palms

     I wait   watch you recede into the dark

follow remnants of the path you left   through settling grains
      seeking your footprints in falling light   stepping
where you stepped   until all fades to black.

Shapeshifter

c.f. Ken Allen (1971-2000)

Humans are: bipedal, users of tools,
deep thinkers with opposable thumbs.
I am a hairy Houdini, born not of Budapest
but of Borneo. An eminent escapologist,
a magician who never reveals his tricks,
nothing up my shaggy, rusted sleeves.
The public love me. The keepers? Less keen.

They take to loitering behind food stalls,
benches, trees. Eyes peeled like a banana.
Walkie-talkies held to their lips like a mango
they mean to eat. Draft in mountain climbers
to scale our enclosure. Eliminate any hold
for a finger or toe. Set camera traps,
microphones. They never catch me escaping.

They try dressing the keepers up as gawkers
sporting bulky Nikons, bumbags, ball caps.
Leave them loitering at the fence in shifts.
But I know the difference, can smell
the wire on them, the forged steel of gates
and hatches. I can wait them out. Eventually,
they grow certain they have defeated me.

As my guards return to fish tank or elephant
house, I disprove this assumption.
Go ambling about the zoo, as you do.
A shapeshifter, interloper, creature
of the in between. I change continent
from hour to hour. Walk through South America,
Antarctica, Madagascar. I like the penguins.

We are what you might have been.
Had you failed in fusing a pair
of chromosomes. An exhibit, a displaced
'old man of the forest', a sackcloth
hatted curio shifting crabwise across
the floor to the piles of food you leave
us, like tribute to some elder god.

Standing on this side of the mesh
I am harder to classify, to contain.
Bipedal, a user of tools, a thinker,
in possession of opposable thumbs.
Here we are: a pair of risen apes.
What separates me from you save
one of those ball caps and a close shave?

Fleet Salvage: Coulthard's Dad

i.m. Walter Coulthard (1925-2002)
Hughie Bell (1925-2015)

i. Portsmouth

We do not set sail to be salvagers. I don't
fancy the Army and my eyes are too weak
for the Air Force to have me. But a fortnight
into training, I'm still turning green, can only
walk crabwise across the boards. Spend my nights
practising under the stars. My days, out at sea,
throwing up overboard. Rounding the forecastle
I pause, Walter Ernest Coulthard's leaning on the rail.
Another Prestonian, a natural sailor, swaying gently
with the swell, the sod might as well be waltzing.
The tug lurches left, sends me thunking sideways
against the bow, I scowl. He turns, already grinning.
"No hard feelings Belly, my dad's a champion
clog dancer and I got my feet from him."

ii. Falmouth

Only two of us made it this far south of Preston.
I can't hate him forever. I'll be stuck with Taffy
weeping at the sight of leeks, Sam and Rufus
arguing the superiority of sheep over pigs,
no one to know what butter pie actually is.
I can put up with him, the great git, if it means
there's another northerner to commiserate with.
Though everything seems easy to Coulthard,

Walt's just another motor mechanic, baby-faced
and big handed, confessing over rum how his first
apprenticeship ended by whacking his bullying boss
over the head with a plank. I gawp, he winks.
"Don't worry, I pulled the swing — only winded him.
My dad's a prize fighter, I got my arm from him."

iii. Plymouth

I, Midshipman Bell, newly minted, wait outside
a bakery whilst Midshipman Coulthard negotiates
on cake. Feeling natty in my dress whites, the hat,
the scarf, the kitbag. The looks from the ladies
might beat even planes, I've got a week of leave
to find out before my ship sails. Minutes stretch,
Walt steps out to a tinkling bell and laughter, arms
festooned with string shopping bags. "You eat
like a bloody gannet, we're only going on the train!"
He frowns, solemn, produces a large Victoria sponge,
breaks it down the middle, offers me a half. I refuse,
watch, horrified, as he eats his way through the other
saying round the crumbs, "My dad won the county
pie eating competition, I got my appetite from him."

iv. Ceylon

Thirteen months after waving Walt off home
to his sweetheart, special license wedding
and choice salvage assignment, Sam hurls
himself into his hammock, sends it swinging

to and fro, pushing off with one sock-escaped
toe. His eyelids blooming algae green under
the browline, sighs, "Bet Coulthard's dad
would've knocked Big Bill out first time."
I measure up in my head, that glimpse of Walt's
father at the Preston Station. Five foot only
on his tiptoes and spats, Bill stomping round
the docks breaking up cadets, pallets, this six foot
in his socks — holey or not — Somerset farmer.
"He's a prize fighter mate, of course he would."

v. Middle of Nowhere, Russia

And I only know that from the cold — and the coffee.
Two months after victory day the clean-up continues,
I've yet to see any parades. Instead, I'm standing
ankle deep in the snow drift that's slid inside
this half-stripped ordnance office north of Moscow.
Contemplating the listing carcass of a filing cabinet
slumped drunkenly against the wall, too heavy
to tilt out of the bunker. Chief Petty Officer Hughes
straightens, scratches his balding head, gives up.
 "We're never gonna get this out of here, empty
the drawers, put it in boxes instead." The fella next
to me — some scrawny cadet from the Casterly,
brand new, the shine barely off him — sighs, shrugs,
says definitively "Coulthard's dad could've done it."

vi. Home Port

I pass him sometimes in town, on the way
to the market or at Preston Guild with Dot
and their three kids, smiling, proud. Filled
out again after the malaria. We talk in passing.
In the end Walt was the salvager, I shuttled
from North Atlantic convoys to Asia, Africa.
Only ever earned a two-month salvage
secondment near the end of the war. Skulking
low in the water off the South of France, found
myself hauling up chunks of the first sea-home
we ever had. Sunk by some other unlucky chump,
who might have had our cabin, run his fingers
over the initials on the underside of the bunk.
WEC, HB, ST, GT. COULTHARD'S DAD WAS HERE.

When I first told Walt all this, we were neither
of us long home, still stretched thin and swaying,
like tall ships run aground on the cobbles
and setts, by the murky waters of Preston dock.
I said "Russia felt a little like that, standing
in that bunker in the middle of nowhere,
gasping like a landed fish, perversely proud
that our joke had run its way around the world.
Ernest Coulthard: prize fighter, clog dancer,
champion pie eater, barely five foot in his spats.
A giant. Crossing countries and continents
in a single bound. Proud, but still wanting to shout —
it's not just words, that's mine, that's ours,
you don't know. You don't know what that means."

Troupe Movements

Prologue

For the last six months of nineteen-forty
London perfects her phoenix impression.
Night after night she takes to the stage,
the old dame dodging enforced retirement.
They're running low on props these days:
ash for facepaint, bone-white pigment
daubed across a chorus of air-raid wardens,
ambulance drivers playing breeches roles.
Lighting is provided by German pyrotechnics,
falling out of cue with the stage directions.
When dawn finally pulls the curtain down
and St Paul's still stands, the audience roars
their approval. An instant hit, it runs and runs,
accompanied by an encore of flame and shrapnel.

Act 1

As December takes its bow, the troupe takes
the hint and — five months before the roof
falls in — exits North, pursued by rent collectors.
The principal cast goes by rail: operatic divas,
prima ballerinas, sardined in second class
with on-leave soldiers. A straggling circus train
of understudies and stage hands takes to the road.
Removal vans, buses and repurposed milk floats
driven erratically by artistic directors (more familiar

with black cabs, the tube, chauffeurs). Stuffed
with scenery, lighting rigs, costume racks, overflowing
sacks of last season's wigs. All aiming northwards
like a compass needle towards the Old Vic's
new home. The Victoria Theatre, Burnley.

Act 2

They make do. Digs are the cramped attics
of millhands' houses. Production runs out
of an office riddled with mysterious mould
and walls with more holes than windows.
The winter revival of outside loos nearly cracks
the courage of elder thespians. The judder
of looms are welcome aftershocks to bones
grown accustomed to constant bombardment.
But the nights are too quiet, the altos gather
in back ginnels at three am to sing themselves
to sleep. Primas practice positioning at the barres
of backyard mangles and Hamlet strides home
from the pub along the mortal coil, by moonlight
and iambic pentameter alone. They settle.

Act 3

Relaunch in the dying days of January. Reduced
in circumstances and size but stretched across
county lines, a proscenium arch from Cardiff
to Carlisle. Their leads lost to a different corps,
the remainder draft dodgers, students on break,

serious Shakespearians past the age of gunfire.
Still, standards must be maintained. Insufficient
stage experience sends Vivian Leigh off with a flea
in her ear — a furious Olivier trailing in her wake.
The director keeps the cat she brought as a bribe.
It makes a nest of the costume box, lingers there,
a panther with Scarlet's eyes. The Vic is embraced,
a novelty, enquired after in shop counter queues,
fate debated alongside shuffling ration coupons.

Act 4

Opening night. Neither variety nor music hall,
no flickering newsreel of the boys abroad.
Beyond imagining with no frame of reference.
Backstage, improvised makeup, lopsided wigs,
lighting rigged by two former biscuit packers,
accelerated out of stage school double quick.
The late addition of a toothbrush moustache
to Richard the Third is vetoed. Curtain up.
A Lancastrian victory seemed appropriate. But,
as the hours pass, the silence is not reassuring.
In London it would be appreciative, pin-drop,
but here they cannot tell. As the closing soliloquy
ends the echo stretches unbearably, then
they raise the roof higher than the bomb could.

Act 5

On the road. Two dramas, one opera, one ballet.
Verdi tours the valleys, where mine overseers

out-sing the tenors. Never before has an opera's
encore been sung by the audience, a Welsh choir
a thousand-strong gathered on a village green.
Margot Fonteyn, fresh from avoiding the Nazis,
is crated up with Verona, Malfi, Elsinore. Skids
down black signposted roads, to mining towns
and mill towns. Pirouetting on cobblestones
and the splintered boards of local church halls.
Brings arabesques to Fleetwood fishwives
who, when next they reach for the gutting knife,
find a leg thrown out behind — counterbalance —
arc backwards from the counter, swan-like.

Epilogue

In early forty-three they return in triumph,
to squat on St Martin's Lane and wait out the war.
The Vic an urchin's playground for years yet.
That first grand jeté on a sprung floor nearly sends
Fonteyn to the barrage balloons. The sopranos
squirm in their silks, the tack of lipstick alien
after a decade of beetroot staining. Romeo takes
to leaning on factory walls, seeking the thrum
of a machine's meter to memorise his lines. In Burnley,
the Victoria crumbles into fragmented memory.
The cat, the costumes, Macbeth declaiming soliloquies
over butter pies. The like of this not seen again until,
in sixty-three, Olivier descends, declares the theatre
'National' again, takes the show back on the road.

Family China

i. Crack

When Ma married my Da — a Protestant —
her father threw her from the house
in a blizzard of books, clothes, makeup.
Flung it all out the upstairs window
alongside enough words to almost fill
the ensuing ten years of silence.
He left her on the pavement,
knelt amidst the peculiar snowflakes
of her belongings, ears still ringing
in the hush that follows an avalanche.

Broken only by the creak of a door,
and her mother, all of five foot four
in her housecoat and slippers, hauling
empty suitcases out onto the cobbles.
Left pocket weighted down by a pilfered
sugar bowl: bone china, rimmed in gold.
Packing done, she pressed this orphaned
remnant of an inherited dinner service
into my mother's outstretched palms;
gifted it as both dowry and blessing.

I arrived a year later, thought nothing
of meeting my grandmother in parks.
Until the age of six, fully believed she lived
up one of Calder Grove's ancient oak trees
with my Aunt Sarah; a sprite-like creature,
just five years my senior, Ma born again
in flaxen haired miniature. The pair
descending only on Sundays, to take tea
with us in a revolving series of park-side cafes.
Out of sight of gossiping neighbours.

ii. Staple

Time — and grandchildren — bank the fires
of grandfather's anger 'til we are allowed
to linger on the edges of family occasions.
Sarah and I remain bound together,
sitting insistently beside each other
at countless weddings and christenings.
Parted only for photographs,
to prevent incessant giggling,
the elbow-driven one-upmanship
of who was taller or better dressed.

Sarah's temper often flared hot, molten,
made of the same stuff as Ma's and mine.
But she learnt from our example to leave
before she was thrown out, in a streetside
snowstorm of her own. Instead, she hid
in our kitchen from a father far stricter
with her than any of her brawling brothers,
popping with righteous fury as she cooled
slowly, 'til the veneer cracked and she wept.
A cycle she repeated again and again until —

on the evening of grandfather's funeral,
my ma and my grandmother share
a glance across the wake's washing-up.
They nod, set aside plate and dishcloth,
draw the kitchen door shut, sealing
us into the sanctity of the confessional.
Eyes lowered, heads bowed, fingers twisting
crucifixes on their chains. It comes out
in fits and starts. Their voices overlapping,
rising, falling, the intonations of catechism.

iii. Restoration

The tale of Ma's wild fifteenth summer
with a friend's handsome, American cousin.
Ma curled over in the yard. Vomit on cobbles.
Then: the enforced silence, a devil's deal
between her priest and her father. A swap.
A daughter for a sister. How often it nearly burst
from her, bubbling out around a glazed smile.
A truth she only screamed once, out on a street,
thereafter confined to the internal echo chamber
of her heart that calcified around Sarah's absence.

The anger builds slowly, steadily like clay
fired in a kiln. As the heat rises our shapes
change. Ma makes us anew. The words stop.
We are still in the kitchen. The suds slipping
from the dishes in the sink. Three generations
of blondes cloistered around a kitchen table.
Only Sarah has moved. The last of Ma's
generation becomes the first of mine.
Backlit, the layered silhouettes in history's
shadow-puppetry show begin to make sense.

A botched weld that held until now, cinched
tight by our grandfather's potter's palms, lies
broken open. Today I have met my sister.
What to do with this carefully wrapped bomb
taped to family china that they have passed
into the hands of our generation? For now,
just keep it cradled between my sister and I,
in our cupped palms under the table. Hold it
as carefully as Ma held that sugar bowl:
paper thin, on the verge of breaking.

Domburg Beach

i.

The sea strips
the sand to strata,
shifts the timeline
on the tides.
The village
was Saxon, was Viking
was Roman.
Was here, then gone.

ii.

One winter reveals
a headless Victory.
She was carried
in triumph
to the church. Left
greening
out of salt until
she was reclaimed,
or lost,
to lightning.

iii.

In harder times
the villagers develop
criminal tendencies.
Wind their way
through the wave
forms of foundations,
the worm casts
of superfluous
underwater wells.
Seek plunder.

iv.

The currents change
on the whim of the weather,
call up
the temple of a forgotten
Roman goddess, plying
her faith amongst
the carcass stalls
of Viking merchants,
the graves of Christians
birthed
out of the mud,
heads facing westwards.

v.

For centuries of dark nights,
the villagers' children
have crept out
through the waves'
boneyard, pillaged the surf's
hand-me-downs
for the brooches and skulls
they liked the best, ferried
them home through
seaweed snares and crab nests.
Of the rest, little is known
and the locals' lips
are salt-sealed.

The Lions of London (1210 – 2014)

Mother slinks out into Whipsnade
paw deep in puddles of English rain,
arches her spine vertebra by vertebra,
grass slick and damp under her nails.
We watch our pride being slowly uncrated,
she washes my ears while we are waiting
in a scentless cave, rough tongue tracing
the faint, water-stained tributaries of veins.
Between conscientious licks, she complains,
"They'd never dare send the ravens away,
the meerkat family are too popular,
even the Humboldt penguins stayed.
But here we are. Packed up, stored away,
hidden on this forgotten satellite campus.
What of the young art student who paid
the entrance fee three times last week,
just to sit by the fence where I laid
and sketch the riverbend of my back,
the fine arch of my forepaws?
What of the children who come in packs of ten,
faces straining to look over the side of our pen
at a dynasty beyond the rule of men?
What about her? What about them?"
Mother snarls, leaves off her licking, rolls
over, sprawls, head tipping into the sunset.
"They have forgotten what we are.
My grandmother once laid in Regent's Park,
watching stars dropping down out of the dark,
like beads of monsoon rain grown large and strange,

striking the soil, the zebras, the hummingbird cages,
sending up sparks with each solid contact.
Felt savannah sun falling, heat singeing the tarmac,
the barb in the end of her mother's tufted tail,
and the tips of her father's dust-dyed mane.
Smelt scattered prey running north to water,
heard their screams as the keepers caught them.
Everything in her said "run" but her parents
did not move, not a whisker, not a claw,
so she stayed, belly down to the concrete, paws
drawn up around her ears. Legend says, her grandfather
came from a London circus, jumped hoops of fire
for an American showman named for a president.
His mother leapt for a whip too, but she was tower-born
as were all those before, the last of those whose blood
was once Barbary, their sumptuous manes black as soot,
their skulls resting at the bottom of the Barbican's moat.
Her parents were sundered from the Bulwark with the rest
of her pride after a monkey bit Lord Wellington's Ensign.
Evicted a scant few years after her uncle died
in a fight with a Bengal tiger and his wife.
Accidentally released by the night-time patrol,
separated only by the application of coal-hot
irons to the tender shell-pink skin of their nostrils.
He died from the wounds shortly after,
like Mary Jenkinson, maid to the keeper,
snuck in one night by a guard who was sweet on her,
for a glimpse of something golden and rare,
found later up in her rooms in the Lion Tower,
lost an arm then her life in the course of an hour.
The Aunt who maimed her lounged below,
licking her lifeblood off her canines and incisors.

It was her grandmother made a friend of Titus,
the King of Spain's prize African elephant,
still seasick from the sail, who crossed continents
to make a match of Philip's Infanta Maria Anna.
Failed, took to drink, guzzled bottles of particularly fine
Charente Cognac, inhaled Malmsey wine a gallon at a time,
was kind enough to save her a trunkful on nights
when a caged life was too dull to be borne.
At least Queen Liz gave us her subjects for company,
saw our value as a symbol, kept us in meat.
Made an event of us for a threepenny bit for the rich,
a reluctantly roped stray-dog or alley-cat
for those more familiar with the Fleet Ditch.
They rarely made it to our plates, raised hell at the gate
when the wind's currents gave them our scent;
our cousin's noses remember what the humans forget.
They darted in to swipe at bare pockmarked shins,
wrested the rope free of sweat-slick palms, fled.
Her uncle, gaunt and black-maned said,
it happened so often they barely flicked an eyelid
to the escaping mongrels who, for all they may get
flattened by a cart or cornered by a bigger, meaner
Tom tomorrow, were still able to run away from their death.
His aunt once kept a dog-dinner as her pet,
its small, warm body curled close under a paw,
rabbit heart rattling pressed up against her chest.
So close it sometimes felt like a milk drunk cub,
whiskers weaved in amongst her own.
Before Bess put us all out on show,
we spent our centuries as a Seraglio,
our charms reserved for Royal Blood only,
our aunts a harem of childless queens,

for the Kings to display to their contemporaries.
Each in their metal grilled receiving rooms, each alone.
Like the Lady Anne, who was once a Queen,
she still walks — headless — around St Peter in Chains,
patrols in cell-paced circles night and day, head
hanging from her belt like a housekeeper's chatelaine.
At her heels, our line of the dust-born lionesses pace,
a disparate pride born of cell dirt and memory.
Mothers, grandmothers, aunts and sisters,
they say, one day, all Tower Queens join her.
Back and back to the first inhabitants
of her royal ancestors' curiosities cabinet.
Encased in a series of stone compartments,
double storied, single celled, the metal grills
of our drawers pulled open for a procession
of lords and ladies, visiting rulers, political
prisoners waiting to hear news of the charges,
the block or the rope, the ruler's mood changes.
A rare treat, but they scared the natives,
who'd never seen spun sunshine, African gold,
rare and roaring creatures prowling out into the cold.
Pacing new cells by paw-lengths, testing
the strength of their teeth on bars of English iron.
They never got very far. The only escapee,
the King of Norway's polar bear, had a head start.
One of the few allowed out on parole,
to swim in the Thames on a long, stout cord.
he cut lazy circles through water, until he pulled
too hard. Snapped his leash, swam home.
The third Henry was impressed by his friend's gift,
but it was not the one that pleased him best.
We were a dowry, three gifts from an Emperor

to a King. A teenage bride in a golden gown,
her southern French treaties, and the lionesses
who stalked in, snarling and wild,
came yawning — roaring — off the heraldry,
the crest he had carried all the days of his house.
Sprang through the doors off the court,
paraded before the wedding party,
singing in their chains of plains left behind
under another sun. But it was his father,
King John, who first loosed us on London,
sent hunters to where we crawled
belly-down across the savannah,
stalking strange two-legged prey
who carried claws in their palms
or at the end of sticks that thrust up
through the long grass like Giraffes' necks.
We followed an easy dinner into nets
and never could go home again.
And though we have often dreamt of it,
we would not go. We are born of London.
In Zoo, Menagerie, Bulwark or Barbican.
For centuries our line has remained, unbroken.
Remember, it was not us who broke trust, but them."

Healing

You go to the National when it rains,
half-empty and echoing, still warm.
Like the kettle Anna left on at home
this morning, your first cup of tea
slowly cooling on the side, before
her shift at the munitions factory.
The children six months gone on
your brother's farm. You list against
the kitchen counter reheating soup —
remnants of last week's meat ration.

Sunny days are saved for Wounded
Admittance to the Zoological Gardens'
shrinking selection of exhibits. The grounds
are moon cratered, lions roaming
a savannah pocked with shell holes.
The rarities evacuated to Whipsnade,
pandas, orangutans and elephants
sequestered away like old masters,
lowered down Welsh slate mines
in dented frames of flaking gold leaf.

The aquarium's closed, leaving only
improvised fishbowls, repurposed
water butts and bathtubs, littering
the floor of the tortoise house. Short
on staff they let you lean against
the rims, scatter food from thick,
bandaged palms, glimpse the bright,

scaled foreigners penned within.
You stop going once your wounds
heal and the fee kicks in again.

Bandage free, your still-ringing
head buys an extra week's leave.
Wandering sandbagged streets,
you glimpse them now and then.
The zebra that ran a good mile
through Camden Town, spooked
by sirens. The bear that stalks
the underground, the crocodiles
slinking through London sewers,
their eyes glinting in the gutters.

Three hummingbirds that flew
out through a hole in their roof
and roosted like jewelled fruit
amongst the fire-warmed ashes
of bombed-out houses. Sighted
one last time a fortnight later.
Coasting on the steam currents
above your waiting Dover train.
Flashes of rare, iridescent colour:
tropical fish, shoaling in a bathtub.

Meeting Myself Coming Back

For Ann Pedder (1820-1849)

Not safe, not 'til you were in range
of the clanging town clock, in sight
of the half-wild wave of your sister.
Who gauged your stumbling gait
from twenty paces, dress ripped,
hat askew, shawl streaming out
behind you like smoke in the wind.
Confused, she stuttered to a stop,
hand outstretched, still reaching
for you: ran. Half carried, half dragged
you, struck dumb and dazed, into town
as the adrenaline ebbed away. Caught
the wide rabbit sheen of your eyes
as words spilled out of your unstoppered
throat onto the constable's desk, fingers
worrying at the dent in your bonnet's brim,
body cooling to shivering, hair tumbling
from its pins, tangled in the tack of sweat.

You name him, he was no stranger,
your eldest sister's former suitor.
Her, married and escaped, he believed
himself entitled to a replacement — you.
An arrest, then a week later, a trial.
The scratches long scabbed over,
you still walk with a limp. Your voice
hoarse from screaming, holds
steady in your recounting and denials.
You do not weep. You do not faint.

His lawyer takes to accusations.
Were you not a former lover, scorned?
Had you not led him on? Were you not
some brightly dressed whore hiding
another assignation with this accusation?
"No I am not." "No I did not." "No, I never would."
Under it all, throbbing like the beat of clogs
at a country dance. "He had no right to me."

His conviction made the papers. The act,
concealed in the euphemistic charge
'assault, with intent etc.', had happened
to a hundred other girls walking back alone
from pubs, mills, church. Was hushed up,
or solved by the communal rough justice
of fathers', brothers', lovers' fists.
A rarity, then, you standing firm, your win.
You were no campaigner — just a milliner,
barely past twenty, motherless, angry.
I hope it did not dim your colours, I hope
you walked that lane again countless times.
A tall, attractive, gaily dressed figure,
with a knife and needles in your basket.

The year is eighteen forty-two, the year
is twenty nineteen, I am heading for my train
on that self-same road, I am meeting myself
coming back. The world has changed.
The world has stayed the same. By now
women have learnt your lessons. We wear
alarms, stay on the phone, carry our keys
split through our knuckles like unsheathed claws.

Through five generations, I may have lost
your height, your sense of style, but I have
retained your colours, your love for hats
and, I hope, your anger. I will think of you
at night, walking home in the dark,
in a body echoing as if it has been
submerged in water, carrying my keys.

Census-Taking

6th June 1841 — 45 Holdsworth Street, Bradford

Birthplace registered as born in county Y/N

The night of: a slinking home, a boarding house,
Mrs McIntyre struggling to fill the forms out,
her ledger not going beyond rent paid and rent owing.
Bed bound guests accosted at the foot of the stairs,
repetitive rhythm of shuttle across frame still echoing
in their ears. A regular by then, only an absentminded,
"Not born in county are you hen?" Shake your head. Later,
pressed beneath the eaves with ten other cotton-lunged
girls, slide awake in the shivering nakedness of Sally Foster's
still-new skin. Horrified at how close you came to truth-telling.

30th March 1851 — 3 Bowling Green Yard, Sheffield

Column added for town and county of birth

Sit, tap the nib on the inkwell's rim, there's little left to fill in.
Beside the children, the husband you acquired seven years
before the first finally died, your line lies blank, waiting.
Time to reclaim what you once shed walking — limping —
down that westward driven crack of a road heading towards
Yorkshire's snaggle-toothed border. The grass stretching out
on all sides. Flat, like a pane of bottle-green glass, marred
only by a bubble six inches off the horizon. A stand of trees,
the desiccated bones of a farmhouse perhaps. Time short,
you did not stop to wonder. Limbs aching, stumbled, tripped,
a bit of yourself slipped from your palms into the rut of a cart
track and you did not miss it for miles. For the first time since
you turned your back to the Stump's long shadow, you feel it,
a wave beaching far inland. Home landing in your lap once more.
Sarah Hardman. Married. Age thirty-four. Place of Birth: Boston.

7th April 1861 — 4 Back Brick Lane, Halifax

The census with the most missing pages

Alice lands in a dosshouse
on Gaol Lane. Practicing
her balancing act, sliding
new names across the tip
of her tongue in front
of the cracked hall mirror.
Head held high, chin tilted,
a little like accepting
Holy Communion, straining
her neck to reach the priest's
fingers, curving up bird-like
to accommodate benediction.
Ann Astor, Phyllis Howe, amen.
She slinks out into Halifax,
in Mary Niles' tender skin,
it pulls a little to smile —
expression not yet worn in.

She turns, collides on the step
with Tom coming in, wrists aching,
nostrils nicked from shaving
with arms stronger, lighter,
than last time he was permitted
use of a razor. "Sorry Missus I—"
"Miss" she says, "just Miss."
He glances down at their hands.
A pale freckled band curled
around her finger, like dust

scattered in that slash of light
that leaks through the slats
in the attic room's shutter.
Scar tissue leans out under
his cuff for a better look. Shiny,
nearly as red as the tips of his ears.
They spend the next six months
learning to lie together, before
sharing this bed in the back-room
above Mrs McGinty's kitchen.
The smell of soup seeping up
through the floorboards
to linger in the bedclothes.
Last week their pillows reeked
of parsnip and leek every time
they turned, seeking the cool
side like the rabbit roasting
on a spit downstairs. Tom Pyne
lodger, Mary Pyne lodger's wife.
Liars and criminals, the pair.

2nd *April 1871 — 21 Cask Lane, Manchester*

Water Damaged

Lord knows you've a fear of forms.
But look at you, forty-one years old,
mother of two, frozen: fingers over
streaming eyes, breathing hard
into the warm alcove of your palms,
holding air close, loathe to let
it leave you. Jack presses his hand
to your shoulder, sends you back
upstairs. Continues into the parlour,
to tell your mother-in-law a tale he wove
whenever someone asked, about a woman
from Bolton who came for the cotton,
met a bargeman half her age and stayed.
On nights like this you wish you were her.

3rd April 1881 — 22 Cunard Street, Camberwell, London

The only page missing on this census

You do not appear on the census in 1871,
longed-for child of a mother thought barren
and a Master Tailor father who could not mend
the hole where you might have been. Then,
after eighteen years of marriage, you come.
They track your days like farmers watch clouds
around the sun, expectant of inclement weather.
They have both come this far before, once.

When the morning of the 3rd of April dawns
your birth has just begun. Your mother paces
upstairs with her sisters, your father waits
below with a pen, fears crossing his wife out,
hopes to pencil you in. The form is fuller
than it has ever been, but there is no column
available for the hoped for, the expected.
He leaves a line blank, chooses not to risk it.

Night falls, labour forges on, the enumerator
has come and gone. On learning of a birth,
he offers to walk the rest of his ward first,
returns here at the end to take a counting
you could still not be added to. You scream
into being in the early hours of the fourth,
dragging London smoke into your lungs:
ash, embers, fumes and all. You both live.

A decade later your house goes missing,
slips out of the record one April evening,
along with five others from your street.
In an archive in some dimly lit warehouse
a weary clerk runs inky fingers through his hair,
and misfiles a page full of truncated lives.
A family of three — no lodgers or boarders —
Head of family, wife and daughter, vanishes.

Another ten years on you have just left home,
Miriam Dodgson. Servant. Twenty. A governess
for two children in the garden squares of Pimlico.
A hundred years later your great grandchildren
will trace their dark hair and twisted lips back
through the generations to you. Without a clue
where you came from, where you've been,
who you belong to. But your parents will know.

5th April 1891 — 48 Shardwell Road, Whitechapel

The first complete census

At two you are with your grandfather,
your mother is pregnant again.
Too small to be of use as a skivvy
to any relatives living closer
they send you where you are loved.
Two hundred miles away in Yorkshire,
you are not the firstborn disappointment.
You are the child named for his wife
who inherited the curve of her cheek,
her chin, the milky blue of her eyes.

At twelve you are with your Aunt.
Your mother has five other children
and you are the toughest to manage.
But your father's sister can find a use
for a girl with the world at her fingertips.
She sets you to work on pairs of gloves
sewing seams by touch. You have no fear
of needles, no need of candles. You sew
all night, an ear tipped to her youngest's
cradle at the first cough. You are useful.

At twenty-two you are in the country.
Your mother sends you to her cousin
after you nearly slip under the wheels
of a hansom cab, whose horses spooked
at a barfight spilling out into the street.
You get lost a lot at first, it's too quiet

and one grain field in the wind sounds
much like another. You rest your hand
in the deep fur between the sheepdog's
shoulder blades, let her lead you home.

At thirty-two you have become your mother,
sitting in her front parlour, waiting
to begin. You are married to a farmer,
carrying a child of your own, your first.
Older than most, you have come home,
you need her. At the first pains she rises,
ushers you upstairs to her bedroom. Trailing
your fingers along the unfamiliar bannister,
you ascend. The next morning, low on sleep,
the clerk fills it in for her, makes a mistake.

Sally Henshaw. Head. Widowed. Fifty-eight.
Mary Talbot. Visitor. Married. Thirty-two. Blind.
Visitor's daughter. As yet unnamed. One day.

31st March 1901 — 14 Tide Waiter's Row, Kirkdale, Liverpool

6 years before The Deceased Wife's Sister's Marriage Act

I am born a dead docker's daughter,
raised in Toxteth Park, Lancashire,
in the lee of the Herculaneum Basin,
thirty years after the Pottery cracked,
petroleum slick in the roots of my hair,
sandstone under the beds of my nails.

I am your wife's widowed sister,
who lost a man to wind and waves
thirty days after I married him,
beached up on your front step
with no children, no pension,
just the clothes I stood in, a smile.

I am your first-floor parlour lodger,
no need for cook or scullery maid,
my sister sacks them all. I will serve.
I sleep by the hearth with the dog
and, on nights when thunder cracks
the casement, your youngest daughter.

I am your fourth child's birth mother.
There is no word for me. No category
to fit me in — ribs, knees, elbows
and all. Compressed down to syllables,
I do not make sense. A lie will have to do.
Anna Louise Ellison. Boarder. Thirty-two.

2nd *April 1911 – 21 Mearsyke, Colne*

The first return completed by householder

Name and surname: Bathsheba Mason.
When my husband suggested we christen
our youngest after me, I lied, said I'd always
hated it. But it was the one thing I'd given you,
after me, after my mother, an old name,
out of fashion now, it might have changed
as you were passed on to other parents.

Relationship to head of family: head —
for this night and the next anyway.
He's staying at his brother's, looking
over the new cattle, sharing more beer,
stinking pipesmoke and glory-day tales
than is good for them, with no thought
to census forms. He'll never read it.

Age as of last birthday: thirty seven.
And doesn't my face show it? Autumn
child, born in my mother's winter years.
The leaves have begun to drop, the bark
to pucker and wrinkle. You were a spring
baby, born on a Tuesday, twenty in May,
with my mother's eyes, my Master's jaw.

Personal occupation: domestic duties.
You could be anything by now. Housemaid,
seamstress, shopgirl, nurse, suffragette.
I gave you up to better than this. Down

on my knees in upper class houses, I dream
of looking in the polished parquet one day,
seeing me seventeen years since gazing back.

Children born alive to current marriage: four.
Count them. Isabel, Harry, John, Hannah Marie.
Ages ten, seven, three and eighteen months.
Number of children who have died — none.
Thank God. Pen hovering over the page,
the truth or the lie? I am Bathsheba Mason.
The number of my children still living - five.

19th *June 1921 — 14 Potato Wharf, Manchester*

Population figures show 2 million more women than men

A decade ago, eight girls hired a room
from an old man who kept a slum
by the canal-side in Manchester.
Paid well for his silence, in shillings
and tanners clubbed together
from satinette purses. Faces flushed
above their collars, eyes flicking
from one alley-end to the other.

The next day, eight girls left home
after breakfast, wandered streets
in ones, twos, threes, sat in museums,
in libraries, on park benches. Drew
disapproving glances from the public,
as they pamphleted on street corners.
Garlanded in violet and green ribbon,
secret-dark eyes shadowed by hatbrims.

That night, eight girls missed dinner.
Told parents they were with friends,
landladies they were with parents.
Gathered in the garret, ate secret feasts
of dubious food from street vendors.
Talked, laughed, planned then slept,
bootheels to hatpins, on mattresses
stuffed tight with straw and mice.

The next morning, eight girls returned,
arm in arm down dawn-lit streets,
hats, skirts and belts askew, hair loose,
scratching bites from some shiftworker's
lice incurred the night before. Triumphant.
Vanishing act complete they reappear,
the other side of the war, the Spanish flu,
the vote. Wives, daughters, mothers once more.

26th *April 1931 — 12 Aqueduct Street, Preston*

All records destroyed during the Blitz

Alfred Hatcher, cotton frame tenter,
will spend this day a decade later
knelt up to his hips in boot-rucked mud.
The belt of a Vickers machine gun
sliding through his palms like cotton,
bullets echoing the shuttle's run.

Millicent Hardacre, apprentice dressmaker,
will prick her fingertips to colanders
angling the collar tabs just right,
gold-threading the eagle of the Third Reich
above a pocket tailored to hide a knife,
map-silk fine as any Saville Row lining.

Terence Blake, Grammar School teacher,
will be using his skills in repertory theatre.
Hacking consonants up the back of his throat,
confidential files clutched under his coat,
running through Dresden alleys low on hope,
dodging dockworkers and late for the boat.

Streets of mill workers, car mechanics,
seamstresses and paperboys. Aspirations
set down in neat rows for the counting.
Abbreviated to childhood notations:
Scholar, scholar, at home, apprentice.
Skip to missing, wounded, widowed, dead.

Acknowledgements

There's never enough room on the page for all who should appear here, but special thanks are owed...

- To my parents, Sue and Paul, for their endless support and enthusiasm in what is often a solitary and somewhat bizarre endeavour.
- To my all my fabulous family. But especially to my grandparents, Walter and Dot Coulthard, Norrie and Peggy Charlesworth, and my great uncle Charles Frederick Pepper, who all would have loved to see the end.
- To my tutors and teachers, too many to name here, for wise words and encouragement: those who can, truly do teach. Particularly to Paul Farley for a decade of mentorship, guidance and supervising my PhD through pretty much everything but the kitchen sink, Polly Atkin for a love of words that overflows to her students and George Kulbacki for putting my feet on the road towards poetry.
- To my friends and frequent first readers, Jess Gofton and Marisa Garanhel, thank you for the laughter, commiseration, and enabling.
- To Bill Swainson for sound advice and a depthless knowledge of poetry.
- To Aaron and the Broken Sleep team for taking a chance on these poems!

Finally, thank you to those who went before me, whose stories and lives inspired and informed these poems.

'Domburg Beach' was previously published at *The Wandering Bard* Feb 2022 https://thewanderingbard.net/2022/02/03/three-poems-by-natalie-sorrell-charlesworth/

LAY OUT YOUR UNREST